U R Enough:
The Ultimate Alphabetized Guide to Boost Your Self-Esteem

International Award-Winning Author
Toneal M. Jackson

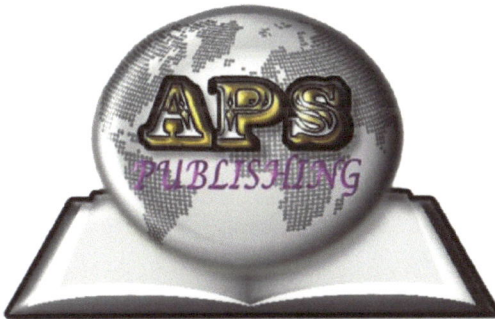

APS PUBLISHING

ISBN: 978-1-945145-79-7

This book is dedicated to my daughters, those I gave birth to and helped raise.

To Autumn, Areana, Angele, Jeriah, Latreana and La'Porscha, I pray you always know that you are enough. Never allow anyone make you doubt yourself or question your value.

I pray I helped instill that message with my words and my presence.

I love you forever

U R Enough:

The Ultimate Alphabetized Guide to Boost Your Self-Esteem

AFFIRM *yourself*

I AM SPECIAL I AM WORTHY I AM ENOUGH

AFFIRM: TO OFFER EMOTIONAL SUPPORT AND ENCOURAGEMENT

We affirm our children. We affirm our significant others. We even affirm complete strangers.
Yet, for whatever reason, we fail to affirm ourselves. Some think that it resembles arrogance or conceit; others consider it to be selfish behavior. Many discount the power that their voice possesses, believing only someone else has the ability to uplift, edify, and empower.

How many times should affirmations be spoken?

At least once a day, but as many times as necessary for them to take effect. Some believe that it takes between three to six months to "rewire" your brain. The more you speak positive, personal statements about yourself, the sooner you rid yourself of the negative imagery that was allowed to form.

REMEMBER, POWER OF DEATH AND LIFE LIES IN THE TONGUE. YOU HAVE THE POWER TO SPEAK LIFE!

A

MAKE A LIST OF 7 AFFIRMATIONS YOU CAN USE DAILY

Sunday

Monday

Tuesday

Wednesday

Thursday

Friday

Saturday

NEGATIVITY

BLOCK: TO PREVENT SOMETHING OR SOMEONE FROM CONTACTING OR INTERACTING WITH YOU

We often encounter negativity. Whether the pessimistic thoughts come from ourselves or others, "stinking thinking" can not only hinder our progress, but it can also improperly shape how we see ourselves. If we base our self-worth upon how much we do, as opposed to who we are (our character), then when we fail to achieve a goal or task, we will believe that we are failures.

This mindset makes it much more difficult to accept the fact that it is still possible to get the job done. We get discouraged and revel in defeat. We become stagnant and ultimately, our growth is impeded.

You must be willing to silence the negative voices - even if they belong to you!

REMEMBER, PEOPLE ONLY HAVE AS MUCH POWER OVER YOU AS YOU ALLOW.

B

THE BEST WAY TO ELIMINATE NEGATIVITY IS TO REPLACE IT WITH POSITIVITY.

Instead of saying everything you can't do, list the things you can.

_____

_____

_____

_____

Instead of focusing on what you've yet to do, list the things you have done successfully.

_____

_____

_____

_____

Instead of dwelling on all the things you dislike about yourself, list what you do like.

_____

_____

_____

_____

CHECK YOUR
CIRCLE

I typically advise people to examine their circle at least every year. This is because people change; some quicker than others. Friendships, like relationships, take work and the older we get, the more responsibilities we are likely to have, so the more valuable our time becomes. Because time is our most precious commodity, we must be intentional in how we spend our time and with whom we spend it.

Too many times we hold on to people like luggage. It doesn't matter if they add value. We don't seem to care if they take more than they give. We simply keep them around because they've always been around.

When we begin to value ourselves, one of the first things we evaluate is how we are or have been allowing people to use us and our time. As we grow to appreciate ourselves, we desire to have others around who will do the same.

REMEMBER, PEOPLE TREAT YOU HOW YOU LET THEM!

C

MAKE A LIST OF THE PEOPLE IN
YOUR CIRCLE. LIST THE REASON
WHY YOU COUNT THEM AMONG
YOUR FRIENDS.
IF YOU FIND SOMEONE WHO
DOESN'T BELONG, YOU HAVE TO
DETERMINE IF YOU'RE STRONG
ENOUGH TO LET THEM GO!

_____

_____

_____

_____

_____

_____

_____

_____

_____

_____

_____

_____

_____

_____

_____

_____

_____

_____

DETOX

DETOX: ABSTAIN FROM OR RID THE BODY OF TOXIC OR UNHEALTHY SUBSTANCES

While we understand the need to physically detox, it is also imperative that we cleanse ourselves mentally, spiritually and emotionally. Oftentimes, we underestimate the capacity of our mind and spirit, possibly because we can't visibly see the negative effects of the overload. If our stomachs were bloated, we'd conclude detox as necessary. Many proactively undergo this process because they understand one of the benefits of cleansing the body is to reset and better monitor what we are consuming.

However, we typically experience burnout, breakdown or something more severe before it occurs to us that we've been overwhelmed and stressed out. It's critical to live a balanced life so you know what it feels like when you're out of balance and are able to do what's necessary to recenter and reconnect with yourself.

REMEMBER, SELF-AWARENESS CAN HELP PREVENT OVERSTIMULATION

D

LIST WAYS THAT YOU CAN AND/OR SHOULD DETOX:

PHYSICALLY

_____

_____

_____

_____

_____

MENTALLY/EMOTIONALLY

_____

_____

_____

_____

_____

SPIRITUALLY

_____

_____

_____

_____

_____

Elevate
Your
MINDSET

Name a dream that you believe is impossible to achieve. If you actually named something, you just proved my point. The fact is the only thing you can't do is the thing you fail to try.

Henry Ford once said, *"Whether you think you can or can't, you're right."* That statement is a testament to the power of the mind. Some believe that where you live or how much money you have determines how far you go in life. The reality is that you have the ability to transform your life simply by how you think.

If you want to succeed (whatever that means to you), you can and will find a way to do so. It may not be easy, but it is possible. There are so many examples of those who rose from the bottom all because they believed they could.

REMEMBER, MINDSET MATTERS!

E

WRITE DOWN SOME THINGS YOU ALWAYS WANTED TO DO BUT NEVER THOUGHT WERE POSSIBLE TO ACHIEVE...

_____

_____

_____

_____

_____

_____

_____

_____

_____

_____

_____

_____

_____

_____

_____

_____

_____

_____

_____

FOCUS on the
FUTURE

How many times do we play the could've, would've, should've game with our lives... ESPECIALLY as we age? I could've been this; I should've done that; if I would've done this, I'd be so much further along.

It's such a dangerous game to play because what good really comes from doing it? Most times, we're left feeling resentful of the choices we actually made, which sometimes causes depression. The fact of the matter is that we can only do what we know to do at the time; we live and learn.

No one has the ability to turn back the hands of time, so all you can do is aim for better moving forward.

Instead of beating yourself up over choices you *should've* made, reflect on lessons you've learned from those decisions. Celebrate the wisdom, knowledge, and growth that resulted. Challenge yourself to find what you can still accomplish now and focus on that!

REMEMBER, YOU CAN STILL CHANGE YOUR NEXT!

F

MAKE A LIST OF THINGS YOU WOULD LIKE TO DO.
JOT DOWN POTENTIAL SETBACKS.
IDENTIFY POSSIBLE SOLUTIONS.

WISH LIST

_____
_____
_____
_____
_____

SETBACKS/OBSTACLES

_____
_____
_____
_____
_____

SOLUTIONS

_____
_____
_____
_____
_____

Give Yourself GRACE

Have you ever noticed that you give more leniency to **other people** than you do yourself? If someone messes up, you typically shrug it off with understanding. However, when *you* do the EXACT SAME THING, you drag yourself through the mud without fail. There is no understanding. All of a sudden, no reason is enough to explain why you were unable to do whatever you deemed necessary.

There **are** times when it was a legitimate excuse. You **were** actually sick. There are only 24 hours in the day, which means, no matter how well you plan, there are still only so many things you can do. The sooner you embrace that, the better. After all, beating yourself up, won't make you more productive. If anything, it'll just end up shutting you down.

TREAT YOURSELF LIKE YOU'RE OTHER PEOPLE

G

WRITE A LETTER TO YOURSELF TO APOLOGIZE FOR ALL THE TIMES YOU WERE UNNECESSARILY HARD ON YOURSELF.

_____

_____

_____

_____

_____

_____

_____

_____

_____

_____

_____

_____

_____

_____

_____

_____

_____

_____

_____

HEAL
from the Inside Out

Life is hard. Many times, it beats you up and you convince yourself to just "roll with the punches". Problem is, punches are painful and can leave bruises.

How many hits have you taken?

Realistically, it's probably too many to count. And whereas that does speak to your resiliency, the question is, How many times did you check to see if those wounds were healed before taking the next blow? Or, did you just put on a bandaid to keep going, acting as though it never happened?

Regardless of how well you can ignore a problem, it's not the same as solving it. You wonder why you've become bitter over the years? It's because you never addressed the root of your pain... You just kept going.

REMEMBER, HEALING IS A PROACTIVE PROCESS

H

LISTED BELOW ARE THE 7 STAGES OF HEALING. IDENTIFY WHERE YOU ARE IN THE PROCESS AND WHAT WORK, IF ANY YOU STILL NEED TO DO.

AWARENESS - Recognizing the need to heal

ACKNOWLEDGEMENT - Accepting/taking ownership of your feelings

FEELING THE PAIN - Safely processing and expressing emotions rather than suppressing them

GRIEVING - Allowing yourself to fully experience (and mourn) the loss

ACCEPTANCE - Acknowledging the reality of past experiences without judgment

FORGIVENESS - Letting go of resentment (towards yourself and others)

MOVING FORWARD - Embracing resilience, growth, and a new chapter in your life

INVEST IN
YOU!!!

INVEST: TO COMMIT MONEY, TIME, OR EFFORT WITH THE EXPECTATION OF RECEIVING A FUTURE BENEFIT

When was the last time you did something for *you*? Bought something *you* liked? Went to *your* favorite restaurant? Watched *your* favorite movie? We neglect ourselves in the name of selflessness, or at least that's what we tell ourselves; but oftentimes, the truth is we simply think more highly of others.

The Bible says that we are to love our neighbor as we love ourselves. So, wouldn't that mean that executing the command properly would necessitate us first loving ourselves? That God's desire is that we find ourselves worthy so that we can, in fact, do right by others?

Investing in ourselves sets the proper foundation. It creates a standard. It tells others that we know how to treat them because we know how to treat us.

REMEMBER, YOU ARE YOUR BEST INVESTMENT!

I

MAKE A LIST OF WAYS YOU CAN INVEST IN YOURSELF.

_____

_____

_____

_____

_____

_____

_____

_____

_____

_____

_____

_____

_____

_____

_____

_____

_____

_____

_____

_____

_____

_____

Journal daily!

Did you keep a diary growing up?
You know the little journal with the lock and key?
The one that you most likely hid under your bed/mattress or in your underwear drawer. Why did you go to all that trouble to write if you were just going to hide it? Because it wasn't about anyone else or their feelings; this was just about you and your feelings.

Although you would have been embarrassed if ever your words were read, the fact is you wrote because it made you feel safe and understood. Writing in that diary provided a positive outlet for expression. Guess what? Just because you may have gotten older, the purpose for journaling hasn't changed. Jotting those thoughts and experiences is empowering because it's not about outside acceptance or validation. Journaling renders an opportunity to note your personal growth and give volume to your voice.

REMEMBER, WRITING HELPS ORGANIZE YOUR THOUGHTS

J

USE THESE PROMPTS TO HELP START YOUR JOURNALING JOURNEY:

MY PROUDEST MOMENT

_____

_____

_____

_____

_____

I DO REALLY WELL WHEN

_____

_____

_____

_____

_____

MY FAVORITE THING TO DO

_____

_____

_____

_____

_____

Keep

GOING....

How many times have you asked someone how they were doing and they responded, "I'm just really going through"? Next time, tell them to keep going.
The reality is that life is filled with ups and downs.
No matter how much money you have. No matter how old you are. No matter how you look. Everyone will have a turn to go through; no one is exempt.

The key is to keep going. Despite how hard. Despite how discouraging or frustrating. Despite how lonely.
Keep going. If you don't stop you will learn a lot about your character. If you keep going, you discover that you are stronger, wiser, and more resilient than you may have ever given yourself credit for being.

The fact is that it takes the obstacles to truly grow you. Anyone can be okay in the good times. But it takes strength and endurance to make it in the bad.

WHEN LIFE HANDS YOU LEMONS, MAKE LEMONADE

K

NAME SOME TIMES WHEN YOU WERE ABLE TO PERSEVERE.

_____

_____

_____

_____

_____

_____

_____

_____

_____

_____

_____

_____

_____

_____

_____

_____

_____

_____

_____

_____

LEARN
from your
mistakes

Tyler Perry says there are no such things as failures; just lessons. If you look at life from that perspective, you might be inclined to live a little more, to try a little more. After all, what's the worst that could happen?

So many people are afraid to do something different because they're afraid they will fail, while others are afraid they will succeed. The reality is that no matter what you do, there's always a lesson to be learned. Once you understand that the lesson **IS** the point, you'll stop beating yourself up and start paying more attention.

REMEMBER, ALL THINGS WORK TOGETHER FOR YOUR GOOD

L

WHAT ARE SOME LESSONS YOU LEARNED AS A RESULT OF YOUR MISTAKES?

_____

_____

_____

_____

_____

_____

_____

_____

_____

_____

_____

_____

_____

_____

_____

_____

_____

_____

_____

_____

MASTER
Your Time

Oftentimes, when we hear about stewardship it's as it pertains to money. But keep in mind that time is actually the most valuable resource as it can never be replaced. Too many times we take time for granted.

I'll just do it tomorrow...

We act as though it belongs to us, as though we are able to foresee the future. This lack of regard for time is what leaves us resentful, and even remorseful.

My grandmother would always say, "Do what you can while you can, so that when you can't, you don't feel bad." If you live by that, you become much more cognizant of and intentional about how you spend your time.

REMEMBER, DON'T PUT OFF FOR TOMORROW WHAT YOU CAN DO TODAY

M

FILL IN THE BLANKS TO SHOW HOW YOU SPEND YOUR DAY.
HAVE YOU MASTERED USING YOUR TIME WISELY OR DO YOU NEED TO MAKE SOME ADJUSTMENTS?

12 AM _____

1 AM _____

2 AM _____

3 AM _____

4 AM _____

5 AM _____

6 AM _____

7 AM _____

8 AM _____

9 AM _____

10 AM _____

11 AM _____

12 PM _____

1 PM _____

2 PM _____

3 PM _____

4 PM _____

5 PM _____

6 PM _____

7 PM _____

8 PM _____

9 PM _____

10 PM _____

11 PM _____

NORMALIZE
SELF-CARE

NORMALIZE: BRING TO A STANDARD CONDITION

If you're 40 and over, the concept of self-care is still relatively new - at least the societal acceptance, anyway. When I was coming up, I didn't hear my mother discuss self-care, much less see her implement it; we won't even talk about my grandmother! No one went to the beauty salon or took a "mental health day".

Instead, what I saw were strong, independent women governing their households. Women who, whether or not they worked a traditional job, ran their own households flawlessly and tirelessly. So, even if not purposely, the lesson I learned was that a woman takes care of her house, her family - everyone except herself. How was she supposed to get rejuvenated? When did she rest? These were answers I didn't find out until my adult years. The fact is that if you don't take care of *you*, you won't be your best for others.

REMEMBER, SELF-CARE ISN'T SELFISH, IT'S NECESSARY!

N

BELOW IS A LIST OF SELF-CARE ACTIVITIES THAT YOU CAN DO FOR FREE...

EXERCISE
(WALKING, JOGGING, YOGA)

SLEEP

MEDITATE

TAKE A BATH/SHOWER

JOURNAL

READ

LISTEN TO MUSIC

WATCH A FUNNY MOVIE

GET A MASSAGE

BREAK FROM SOCIAL MEDIA

PAINT

SPEND TIME WITH LOVED ONES

Own Your FEELINGS

So often, we feel as though we have to shrink for others to grow. The reality is that you don't have to be less for someone else to be greater. You can have your own voice and opinions, while respecting those of others.

How many times do you forego a response because you didn't want to hurt someone's feelings? Even if and when your silence costs us you your peace? My point here is not to incite arguments or discord, but rather to encourage the belief that your feelings matter, too.

You are just as important as the person whose feelings you honor. You should be surrounded by people who value you and your feelings. When you own your feelings, you show yourself that you matter.

REMEMBER, SPEAKING UP FOR YOURSELF BUILDS CONFIDENCE

O

USE THESE PROMPTS TO HELP COMMUNICATE YOUR FEELINGS:

I'M HAPPIEST WHEN

_____

_____

_____

_____

_____

_____

I GET ANGRY WHEN

_____

_____

_____

_____

_____

I FEEL DISAPPOINTED WHEN

_____

_____

_____

_____

_____

PLAN FOR SUCCESS!

PLAN: DECIDE ON AND ARRANGE IN ADVANCE

"If you fail to plan, you are planning to fail."
Benjamin Franklin

Everyone defines success differently. For some, success may be getting married and having a family. For some, it may be graduating from college. Others may say earning six figures, while others may say being debt free means one is successful. Regardless of how you define it, one thing is for sure - in order to obtain it, you must have a plan.

Notice, I didn't say you had to have a goal. Setting goals have been a distraction for generations. It gives a false sense of satisfaction because you've stated what you will do *some* day. Without a plan of execution, steps you will take to actually achieve your goal, some day will never come.

REMEMBER, THERE'S A DIFFERENCE BETWEEN A GOAL AND A PLAN

P

MANY PEOPLE HAVE GOALS THAT THEY NEVER ACHIEVE. THAT'S BECAUSE THEY FAIL TO CREATE ACTIONS STEPS TO EXECUTE. LIST *ONE* GOAL BELOW ALONG WITH ITS CORRESPONDING EXECUTION PLAN(S) FOR:

REMAINDER OF THIS YEAR

_____

_____

_____

_____

_____

THE NEW YEAR

_____

_____

_____

_____

_____

_____

_____

QUIT
MAKING EXCUSES

There are certain things in life that are beyond our control,
no matter what we do, how we feel, or what we possess,
it's not enough to alter the way certain situations will go.
But then there other are things we can control.
And when we choose not to do those things that will help
benefit us, or positively effect the outcome,
we must deal with the consequences.

I don't feel like it. I'll get around to it later.
I just don't have what it takes.
These are all excuses.

Who **EVER** feels like it? How you feel should not limit you.
Obviously, if you have a bonafide illness, that's not what I
mean. But those who roll over in bed and refuse to get up,
and then complain because the hours in the day
have passed by… Your later has left.
And if you apply yourself, it will indeed happen.
It may not be easy, but it is possible.

REMEMBER, HARD ISN'T A REASON NOT TO TRY

Q

NAME AN EXCUSE YOU MADE THAT HAD DIRE CONSEQUENCES.

_____
_____
_____
_____
_____
_____
_____
_____
_____
_____
_____
_____
_____
_____
_____
_____
_____
_____
_____
_____
_____
_____

Respect
YOURSELF

RESPECT: TO ADMIRE SOMEONE'S ABILITIES, QUALITIES, OR ACHIEVEMENTS

An age old debate poses the question:
Which is more important, love or respect?
Many, including myself, believe that respect creates the foundation on which to build love.

Oftentimes, you believe that if you do what others ask, with no regard for yourself, it will give them to like (or even love) you. What is not factored into the equation, however, is whether they will respect you. Without respect, people will fail to consult you about practical and important matters. Why? Because they know you will simply defer to their judgment, so why bother.

So, how do you get others to respect you? Let them see that you respect yourself. That you have standards. Lines people aren't allowed to cross. When they see that, even if they don't like you, they'll respect you.

REMEMBER, RESPECT ISN'T GIVEN, IT'S EARNED

R

LISTED BELOW ARE THINGS YOU CAN DO TO HELP BUILD SELF-RESPECT

IDENTIFY YOUR VALUES
What matters to you?

STOP NEGATIVE SELF-TALK
Replace insults with compliments

SET HEALTHY BOUNDARIES
Establish guidelines for how you want to be treated and learn to say "no"

FORGIVE YOURSELF
Let go of past guilt and shame

SPEAK UP FOR YOURSELF
Assert your needs when interacting with others

CELEBRATE YOUR ACHIEVEMENTS
Acknowledge and celebrate your successes without the need to receive validation from others

STOP DOUBTING *YOURSELF*

Why do you doubt yourself?
I get it. You've made some bad, or at the very least, questionable decisions in the past. But who hasn't? So, again I ask, Why do you doubt yourself?

You've grown so accustomed to beating yourself up that you can't fathom that maybe you could be right this or the next time. But you gotta build a bridge and get over yourself. There won't always be someone to tell you the answer or lend a helping hand. So, you must learn to stop doubting yourself and make the hard decisions.
Even if you don't get it right, you can learn the lesson.

REMEMBER, PROGRESS BEGINS WHEN DOUBT ENDS

S

WHAT MAKES YOU DOUBT YOURSELF?

_____

_____

_____

_____

_____

_____

_____

_____

_____

_____

_____

_____

_____

_____

_____

_____

_____

_____

_____

_____

_____

_____

_____

TRUST
THE
PROCESS

TRUST: BELIEVE IN THE RELIABILITY, TRUTH, ABILITY, OR STRENGTH OF

If you are consistent in what you're doing, over time, your hard work will pay off. The problem is that for you to believe that the process will work, you need to believe in the one participating *in* the process. You must have confidence that you can do what you are attempting or even thinking to do. But, if you understand that you're not the one you're depending on, it makes things a bit easier.

There's a scripture in the Bible (Philippians 4:13) that says, I can do all things through Christ that strengthens me. Simply put, with God all things are possible. So, next time you attempt to do something, ask God to take the lead and order your footsteps. You'll no longer be trusting you, but the one who makes all things possible.

REMEMBER,
YOU DON'T HAVE TO SEE IT
TO BELIEVE IT

T

WHAT IS ONE OF THE MOST CHALLENGING PROCESSES YOU'VE ENDURED?

_____

_____

_____

_____

_____

_____

_____

_____

_____

_____

_____

_____

_____

_____

_____

_____

_____

_____

_____

_____

_____

Utilize Your Gifts

Everyone is born with a gift. The strange thing is many underestimate their gift because they don't see others possess it. So, they hesitate to share their gift - even downplay or deny it when asked.

What you must realize is that everyone isn't purposed to do the same thing. Your gift is what makes you unique, what makes you special. It wasn't meant for you to do or be the same as others, nor is it meant for them to be a carbon copy of you.

Embrace your gift - regardless of what it is.
Utilize your gift to help others. It will in turn benefit you.

REMEMBER, IF YOU DON'T USE IT, YOU'LL LOSE IT

U

WHAT GIFT(S) DO YOU POSSESS? HOW DO YOU UTILIZE YOUR GIFT(S) TO BENEFIT YOURSELF? OTHERS?

_____

_____

_____

_____

_____

_____

_____

_____

_____

_____

_____

_____

_____

_____

_____

_____

_____

_____

_____

VALUE
Yourself

It seems like common sense to say, Value Yourself.
If it were that easy, everyone would do it.
Although everyone *should*, the reality is that many people don't. Typically, the reason is they were never taught. Being taught doesn't just look like sitting in front of a chalkboard (whiteboard) and repeating, *I am valuable*.
It looks like having your foundational figures - parents, family, friends, etc. pour into you;
edify you simply because of who you are.

Learning to value yourself starts with knowing that you are valuable. Not the things you own, or how you give of yourself, just who you are as a person is valuable. Why? Because it's only one of you. When you see yourself as valuable, you begin to carry yourself differently because you understand there is no replacing you.

REMEMBER, YOU ARE A MASTERPIECE IN PROGRESS

V

WHAT DO YOU LIKE MOST ABOUT YOURSELF?

_____

_____

_____

_____

_____

_____

_____

_____

_____

_____

_____

_____

_____

_____

_____

_____

_____

_____

_____

_____

_____

_____

Welcome
NEW IDEAS

It's been said insanity is doing the same thing
and expecting different results.
As you grow and evolve, you learn to welcome new things.
New places. New people. New ways of doing.

You get to a point where your focus is not on whether *you*
had the right answer or if *your* idea was selected. As you get
older you want to work smarter and not harder.
You realize there is so much information and so much that
you never heard of or even knew existed.

Over time, you learn to stop internalizing everything.
Your focus becomes on getting the job done as effectively
and efficiently as possible. If that means using a new idea,
then so be it.

**REMEMBER, EVERYTHING
BEGINS WITH AN IDEA**

W

LIST SOME IDEAS OF WAYS THAT YOU CAN POSITIVELY CHANGE YOUR LIFE.

_____

_____

_____

_____

_____

_____

_____

_____

_____

_____

_____

_____

_____

_____

_____

_____

_____

_____

_____

eXamine

EXAMINE: INSPECT IN DETAIL

I always say, your mindset matters.
How you see yourself, the world, and yourself in the world
will determine your approach to executing your purpose.
You have the choice as to how things and people effect you.
You may not be able to control what happens but you can
control your perception and your reaction.

It's necessary to maintain realistic expectations.
Many times, it's not always what happens, it's what we
expected in relation to what actually occurred.
If you know what to expect, you won't be (as)
disappointed with the outcome.

Be sure to surround yourself with people who can help you
develop a proper perspective of life. Mentors, spiritual
leaders, counselors, etc. are typically unbiased in their
world view. They can help ensure that your outlook is one
that will help enrich your life.

REMEMBER, HEAR ALL THINGS BUT CLEAVE TO THAT WHICH IS GOOD

X

THINK ABOUT YOUR PERSPECTIVE OF LIFE. WHAT ARE SOME OF THE BENEFITS OF YOUR OUTLOOK? WHAT ARE SOME OF THE DRAWBACKS?

_____
_____
_____
_____
_____
_____
_____
_____
_____
_____
_____
_____
_____
_____
_____
_____
_____

YIELD
GROWTH

A sure fire way to boost your self-esteem is to get things checked off your to-do list. Once you get going, it makes you feel good about yourself and your potential.
The more you do, the more you believe is possible.

How frequently should you produce results?

You should aim to produce something fruitful everyday.
It's not about how fast you work or how much you get done; what's most important is your consistency.
The fact that you're chipping away at your goal daily.
After all, slow and steady wins the race.

Ultimately, what you're doing is creating best practices for success. It will have a domino effect. The more you accomplish in one area of your life, the more you will want to accomplish in other areas of your life.

REMEMBER, PRODUCTIVITY IS CONTAGIOUS

Y

IDENTIFY SOME WAYS IN WHICH YOU HAVE GROWN THIS YEAR.

_____

_____

_____

_____

_____

_____

_____

_____

_____

_____

_____

_____

_____

_____

_____

_____

_____

_____

_____

_____

ZERO IN ON

WHAT MAKES YOU YOU!!!

As you grow in your journey to self-worth, it's great to spend time alone. This helps you to become more acquainted with yourself. You probably have your flaws and shortcomings memorized, but now, you must focus your attention to EVERYTHING about you. You must be willing to accept the fact that you're not all bad; in fact, you probably have A LOT that's great!

Getting to know yourself is very rewarding. It helps give you an appreciation of all you have to offer. You learn that it may be traits you have you didn't realize you possessed because others may not talk about it.

When you spend so much time focusing on others, it's easy to lose yourself. Spending time alone gives you a chance to discover things about you that you may have forgotten. Things that may make you smile.

REMEMBER, BE YOURSELF; EVERYONE ELSE IS TAKEN

Z

MAKE A LIST OF YOUR UNIQUE CHARACTERISTICS, TRAITS, AND TALENTS.

_____
_____
_____
_____
_____
_____
_____
_____
_____
_____
_____
_____
_____
_____
_____
_____
_____
_____
_____
_____
_____
_____

Toneal M. Jackson

Empowerment Specialist, Toneal M. Jackson is an international award-winning author, publisher, and filmmaker. She's also a transformational speaker, coach, podcaster, and singer. Her business, Educated and Empowered, equips authors, women, and entrepreneurs with the information and inspiration to be their best selves.

Toneal is a First Lady, evangelist, and president of the Women and Outreach Departments at her church, Carol Divine Temple. She has been married for over 20 years. Together, she and her husband have five daughters and one grandson.

Other Books by Toneal include:

Pleasing Your Partner:
A Spiritual Guide to H.A.P.P.I.N.E.S.S.
Four Girls: A Lot of Choices
It's A Way to Say It All:
How to Communicate with Your Partner
It's A Way to Say It All:
How to Communicate with Your Kids
Inspiration from A.B.O.V.E.
Growing Up to be Happy
She's Out. I'm In.
Four Girls Learn Their Colors
Learning to Love Me (anthology)
Being an Authorpreneur:
How to Succeed in the Book Business
Love Me... Please
Praying Peace over My Life
Praying Purpose for My Life
Praying Problems out of My Life
Praying Prosperity into My Life
The Race to the Ring (anthology)
The Fruit of the Spirit (anthology)
Being A Black Man... It's Harder than You Think

www.ingramcontent.com/pod-product-compliance
Lightning Source LLC
LaVergne TN
LVHW010028070426
835513LV00001B/17